GIFTED

MAIA BROWN-JACKSON

Nymeria Publishing LLC

First published in the United States of America by Nymeria

Publishing LLC, 2025

Nymeria Publishing

PO Box 350747

Jacksonville, Fl 32235

Visit our website at www.nymeriapublishing.com.

Print ISBN 9781969098024

Ebook ISBN 9781969098031

1st Edition

Printed in U.S.A

This collection is for those astounding, wonderful people who patiently, stubbornly kept loving me despite my attempts to set them free of such a god-awful burden with never-ending (apparently annoying) arguments as to why I didn't deserve it. Thank you all for helping me learn to believe in myself.

Table of Contents

Acknowledgements: "I heard Esther call," and excerpts of "Holy," "Delicate fools," and "Sitting shivah" are all updated versions of poems featured in And My Blood Sang (Tim Saunders Publications, November 2023). "Into the fire" was featured in the anthology Remembering Audre Lorde (Moonstone Press, February 2024). "Funerary rites" includes an updated excerpt of "Haunted; still alive," featured in the anthology International Women's Day 2024 (Moonstone Press, March 2024). "Canary in the coal mine" includes an updated excerpt of "Holy II," featured in the Spring 2024 BlazeVOX Books journal. "St. Jude" was featured by Rising Phoenix Press in September 2024.

INTRODUCTION

Necessary definitions: "A Greek Chorus is a theatrical device originating in ancient Greek theater involving a small group of performers—who are usually unrelated to the central action of a story—commenting on the central action of a play. The chorus speaks directly to the audience and may not interact with the main characters of a story at all." – Masterclass, *2021*

Coryphaeus: "The leader of the chorus in ancient Greek drama."– Collins Dictionary, *2019*

Necessary-only-to-the-overly-pedantic-dickish-or-otherwise-frustrating reminder: This is not a play, nor is it ancient Greece on or off the page. This is a fantastical collection of poetry about a girl raised to sacrifice herself to save a dystopian world who has a strange relationship with Death, who Itself can only appear outside of the metaphysical confines of poetry. Yes, there is a chorus, and yes, it acts a bit strangely, and yes, the social and political themes you note are intentional. The poet is going to have fun now; please suspend disbelief.

Unnecessary addition meant to keep you from worrying overmuch: This is *not* a tragedy.

IT IS ABOUT TO BEGIN, IT IS BEGUN ALREADY: AN OVERTURE

I met Death at an unspecified time

The coryphaeus, saunters in as dramatically as possible,
leading the other members of the chorus.
It is not really a theatric entrance onto the page, though,
and this is not really the moment they wanted to arrive,
while we briefly exist outside space and time.
But it is now begun.

The chorus do not look directly at the Thing with the girl.
It's only almost visible if you
catch a glance in the periphery of your vision.

I always equated the dark with monsters,
with the nothingness I had been told came *after*,
with hands and claws always just out of sight,
ready to grab.

And I knew that a piece of that darkness
lived within me
and as I grew,
so did the darkness.
So I hid it deep inside
and devoted myself to pouring out
all the light I could find
and all the magic I could create
to everyone I touched
until I had emaciated what little I had inside.

I was too wary to trust myself,

too afraid of what I might be, deep down.
I feared my defenses might crumble:
but I would hold it back as long as I could,
covering it with an overabundance of selflessness.

I said yes,
and yes,
and yes again,
again,
always;
it became too much.

I had given too much.
Then there was nothing left but that seed of darkness.
That little piece of Death.

So I decided to cling to It instead,
to embrace what had survived
the yeses and
the corrosion and
my own attempts to smother It
and I was told,
No.
This is not your existence.
But it is your power.

But it scares me, I said.

I know, Death replied.
That's because you think of only the endings,
not the beginnings.
All you humans, so frightened of change
that you'll slave away in misery
just to keep the lights on.

Because you can never see past an ending.
Your power is not that you were told to be a hero—
remember *that* always—
and not that you were told to overcome darkness,
but that you can bring about an *ending*.

There's nothing after the end, I said.

No, said Death.
There's not what once was.
But there is something new.
You've always been afraid
because you are change, and
change means never knowing what comes next.
It means that all you'll have,
in each instant, is yourself.

I realized that Death was telling me
something I had always known deep inside:
that the dark was never the power of nothingness.
It was the power to create something new,
and only very few knew it wasn't something to fear,
and I could be one of them.

That was—terrifying? Exciting?

The world has fought against me very hard
because it likes the status quo, Death said.
It is afraid of change.
But a new age will dawn, and you can rise—

I thought of the yeses
and I thought of change,
and I wanted to say,

I have seen evil,
and I vow to change the world,
but I couldn't force the words from my throat.
I was already born a girl.
What role did I play if not one of sacrifice?
If not one of offering,
yielding,
until the very end?

(I didn't realize, not for a long time,
that Death was also trying to warn me,
trying to be the Friend I wasn't allowed
to have as a champion.)

(I didn't realize, not for a long time,
that choosing kindness
would, too, have a cost.)

BORN AS SACRIFICE

February

I was born with Death's fingers wrapped
around my neck,
a family curse that tried to take me, too.

Chorus: Death, of course, had a different explanation.
Death needed her attention—
you know why—or, you will—
but everyone was so delighted she survived long enough
that she might become a sacrifice later on
that Death realized It had to be more clever
in the future if It wanted to talk to her.

As a child, my existence was celebrated.
As an adolescent, I was rushed past such folly,
ignoring February entirely,
and ran straight for spring,
spending the dark, cold months
trapped solely in learning what was to come.

Chorus: Remember,
Death did try to caution her.
But it's hard to unlearn
that which we've always accepted,
and this is just the start of the story.

As a young woman they taught me
the most important lesson:
I was born in the darkness, in the cold,
in this *world*,
and I survived it all.
Thus in the midst of cruelty,
with a scythe pressed to my flesh,
nothing can truly scare me now.
(Except myself.)

Girl as temporary

I don't know when I first learned
that my purpose in this world
was to sacrifice my life
so that others might live theirs.

I don't know why I didn't ask,
Why does girl mean give?
Why does it mean loss?
I didn't understand that our surrender
to the greater good
was the only reason
some of us girls were so special.

They told us we were heroes.
They told us we would save the world.
They told us we were *good*.
They didn't tell us if we would
still be here to see what came next.

Delicate fools

And yet.
There are still those fools
who call girls delicate,
protected,
naïve.
Let me ask:
how young were you
when you first learned
to remove blood
from a white bedsheet?

Our bodies have never been
our own to control.

When I was younger,
I thought perhaps it was sewn
into the lining of my every jacket,
the hauntings of tragedy that I carried
with me like a second shadow.

But I stripped myself bare
and presented my naked flesh
to the world, reminding it
I was just another human,
and still the weight of obligation
did not leave me:
the price for this world
—that loss of girlhood,
that futility of imagining a life grown—
was cemented.

I could feel nothing.

It was never mine to offer

No one ever called my youth precious,
nor tried to preserve my innocence.

I'd seen children get kissed on knobby knees
while I was learning to endure alone
because I knew I couldn't count on anyone,
not later,
not when the time came—

No. I had to cede my time as child
because someone else offered the
part of my life known as "girl."

Chorus: Yes, it is almost always girls this happens to.
No, it is not every girl.
How would society continue then?

In this world, girl *simply means one who will never have*
the opportunity to survive long as woman.

I didn't have to ask if the abnegation
and constant surrender to the neverending
asks *(they were never* "asks"*)*
were my purpose.

I remember the realization coming in bits and pieces,
first just losing viscera and gore—
and that happened much more frequently

than some men might realize—
and then I was resigned to the intimate knowledge
of my anatomy and its flaws
long before most my age knew that
it one day would all end in dust.

(And they never told me,
not to my face,
but there were whispers
that my time was going to be
shorter than most.)

Into the fire

As a little girl,
I was raised deafened by goodness,
struck silent by ideals,
blinded by justice.

As a little girl, after all,
I wanted to be good.
I was *raised* to be good.

And that means when I am given a choice
I still run directly into the fire every time,
and I've become scorched forevermore,
flames peeling away any place
I once had left to hide.

I know they can see me burning
and they can't stop it,
and they always knew
this was how it would end.

I am who they raised
and they trained me well.

The other girls wish
I had not taken it all so much to heart,
and I wish the same for them—

and they know I'm sorry,
(I'm so sorry)
but I am going to choose the fire every time.

Chorus: And for that, despite their sorrow
they understand.
They, too, were raised just the same.

Funerary rites

Some girls are born with halos
and some are born in flame.

Some wanderers have broken wings
and some fighters bare their fangs.

I can hear the words spreading;
though we were not *friends*—
we're not expected to be here for very long
so they never bothered overmuch
with teaching us to socialize—
we have our rituals.

Us girls have jaws of steel
and blood dripping from our lips,
comes the rejoinder of still more voices
(enough that no affect, no tone, comes through)
from girls not sacrificed that day:
We will drink your blood like wine.

For as long as we are haunted,
we know that we're alive.

RAISED AS HERO

But what does Atlas deserve?

> Chorus: Atlas, we might have called her once,
> but now we say, drop your arms.
> There's no point, the world is burning already
> and
> you might as well let it fall.

Atlas,
aren't your arms tired?
Did you make this choice yourself?
If someone took your burden,
what would you do with your life?

> Coryphaeus: Don't forget this:
> it's important.

> Chorus: Come now, you're not Atlas,
> and the fate of the world can't rest
> on your shoulders alone.
> Do you remember how young you were
> when you first thought it did?
> When you first believed you deserved less,
> deserved nothing,
> but had to earn each inch of space and breath of air?

Yes, I could say easily,
yes, I remember
when I was raised
to abandon my own life in a heartbeat:
when I was born a girl.

Saint Jude

All my life I've been told,
yourturntofight
(for what?)
andpush
(against everything)
and by now Saint Jude's got nothing on me
because I'm drawn to lost causes
like bang(!)
match and flame
and oil, kerosene—
in my veins, under my skin,
thrumming and turning red
when exposed to oxygen
so I can't even breathe
and—

and still
they ask for more—

and—!

Where I stand

Standing here, alone:
a glass cannon with one shot left.
After all, who defends the weapon come alive?
When I was small and inexperienced,
all they saw was glass
that had to be protected
until it was made bulletproof.
So I was hidden,
treated as a fragile thing,
until they could determine my purpose;
until I could bruise and bleed and burn
and carry on without complaint.
When my true shape proved to be
unlike theirs but instead even more than they'd hoped,
something that could wreak havoc upon their enemies,
there was no longer a need for tending.
I can still shatter—
despite my training and my fortitude
I am made up of the same soft flesh as them
and that they do seem to purposefully ignore—
but until I do I will continue to plant my feet and stand tall
where I always have:
between them and the danger.

I questioned

Don't tell, alright?

> *Chorus: We won't, we promise.*
> *We are merely here to witness*
> *and occasionally explain or react,*
> *as your story is yours alone,*
> *completely alone,*
> *and you have no companion save for Death.*
> *So speak to us as you will.*

When I was young
I asked why there was this chasm growing
between what I had begun to want and
what I was told I would become.
I asked myself to no avail,
and then the void of night.

You were born under the wrong star,
it answered.
You want to love, but
you have to fight.

I don't want to—

gogogo

please, please
just let me—

lovelovelove

The drum beats in my chest
no matter how I try to stifle it
as it whispers,

fightfightfight

*The chorus shifts uncomfortably amongst themselves,
knowing their role, like yours, is merely to watch, not act.*

I heard Esther call

You carry Death close,
it was said.
It's in your blood.
You hear that screaming?
It's your ancestors saying,

We tried to help,
and we were massacred—
Daughter,
take care—

you will never be safe.

It's in my lungs.
It burned, and
it blackened me inside
when thousands were slaughtered.

It's in my brain.
Darkness, curling ever closer,
round the amygdala,
sliding closer to the frontal lobe,
taunting me,
as I struggle to quell its cry.

Death has watched and waited
as I've grown into a worthy sacrifice.

We know you're tired, daughter,
the women croon to me at night,
but your fight has just begun.

We know it hurts,
the saints whisper through
the gale that steals my breath,
but isn't that why we resist?
We saw and we wept and we sacrificed
and—

   Stagger to your feet, girl,
I hear the wolves whisper.
   Shove those organs back inside
   and press tight, tight, tight
   until your veins and arteries
   follow your orders once again.

   Pull yourself together, girl.
The howl whips around me,
carried by the biting wind.
   Your battle isn't over yet.

   You are a warrior.

I'm not a warrior,
I protest in vain.

   You are a warrior.

I am a girl. I am soft.
(I am lying; even were I
without my destiny,
why should my girlhood
make me *soft*?)

They're baring their teeth at me,
laughing.

You're a girl. You're soft enough to live.
You're strong enough to be alive.
You're a goddamn warrior.

Act like it.

Death scratches at my wrists
and tells me,
<u>I am here for you, child,</u>
<u>but remember:</u>
<u>you have but this brief time before</u>
<u>you and I depart together for good.</u>

My knuckles are bloody
and my lip is split
and my spine is bruised.

I scream at the women who sacrificed themselves
untold times before because
I never wanted to fight.
I never asked for this—
I never asked for *life*—

More than girl...?

Never familiar with gentle,
nor with getting what
I won't admit I want,
I began to wonder,
if maybe, just *maybe*
there was something in me
that was more than "just" a "girl."

Chorus: Should you hold your breath?
Is she beginning to understand?
Does she want something more?

After all, how can they expect
a "girl" –and what's wrong with "girl"?—
to save the world all alone?
How much will my sacrifice cost
anyone but myself, anyway?

The price of humanity
never did run that cheap, though,
and as much as they love a hero,
they've never cared much for a "girl."

Chorus: No, just let it out again, disappointed.

26

STRUGGLED AS HUMAN

Holy

I tire of being human:
I wish to be holy.
My hands, bless not bruise—
my mouth, sing not sin—
my heart, unbroken with purpose,
just like they promised me
I would be as a savior.

It doesn't make much difference,
though.
My time is limited here,
and no matter if I bruise
or bless,
no matter how much I believe,
I am human
and
(somehow)
I will do what I must before it's over.

Not girl

I wish I were a shapeshifter.
In my dreams, I am
not "girl" but

wolf,

lion,

beast.

In my dreams,
I am born free and
unburdened,
and neither my
fangs nor my mistakes
cause any call for attention.

In my dreams,
as I race to the cliff's edge
and hurl myself at the stars
and whatever anomaly
they chose me for
will stop gravity itself.

"Girl" will become my battlecry,
and I will hear it echoed by
those same ones who
chose me for *this*.

(I'll still save them all the same.)

This prison of flesh

I punish my body for being human.
I'm sure I was supposed to be something more.

The flaws disgust me:
the birthmarks, the freckles,
the flush on my cheeks,
the shadows under my eyes,
the wildness in my hair.

I want to be a different creature,
a more perfect one.
I want to be marble, and ivory, and silk.
Every signifier of our humanity can be considered deficient.
Every defect is a vulnerability in the right circumstances.
Or the wrong ones.

The ones who told me who I am now—
I wasn't raised to be a mere human.
I was raised to save the world.

At the least, shouldn't people call me
wretched,
not *beautiful*?
Shouldn't they wonder about the stories behind my scars,
and see each as another battle I won?
Another survival?
Not a flaw to be covered in those rare times
something other than my fate takes precedent, when
they care about my appearance?

Let me strip naked, and proudly tell of
each time I thought I was going to die,

and each time I proved again my incredible strength
despite this fragile form.

I wish it were true that destiny
could give me something *more* than this.
I dislike being confined to something as frail
as this sack of meat.

Some people say our bodies are mere transport.
So I exist, corporeal, for my brain? soul? heart?
Nonsense. I exist for battle.

And yet
why shouldn't I get to enjoy the physicality of life,
the pleasures of the flesh?
Why should I insist I detach, separate,
keep myself apart?

I look at the world around me,
and so often I don't want to be part of it.
I don't want to be one of these angry, petty, sweaty beings
that roams the land, killing the earth and each other—
as if I had a choice.

I would give my life in a heartbeat for humanity.
But is that because I believe in its potential,
or because I'm so accustomed to being asked for blood?

So here I am, trying to make peace
with this carcass-not-yet-dead filled with saline,
when I wish to still exist half burning stardust,
half untethered atoms—

Anemic

Chassis is now nothing more than
metaphor; not personal, not pleasurable,
just a mere tool for use.

Just paper thin skin over
blue trails
that always bruised too easily,

Chorus: The public don't like to be reminded of mortality.

and I wish for more of the
iron born in dying stars
(because something must always end,
mustn't it,
for something new to begin?
If the star is already going out,
why can't it at least help me hide my wounds?
Or is that how people think of me:
already mortal, might as well save the day?)

*Chorus: Why can't she see the difference between
living, growing, changing girl
and clouds of gas amidst lightyears of empty space?
Why does she so admire the latter?*

That is my purpose, isn't it?
I am here, I was born, I live
so that I might hurt and hurt
and hurt
and die.
And others will survive.

(I suppose then that
the bruises don't matter much.)

Midas' daughter

The blue road maps crawling up my arms
belie the redredred blood that has been staunched
time and again,
turned violetjadeamber bruises,
staining my skin.

Chorus: The heroes start fighting young.

What they can't see is that my blood
has turned liquid gold,
that I have been broken and rebuilt so many times
that I am mutable; I am molten.

Chorus: Not everyone bothers to consider them human.

I am not the girl who inhabited
fair, soft, unscarred skin,
and I no longer wear that girl's skin,
not for many years now.

I am heavy, I am soft, I am precious;
I have been rebuilt like the ship of Theseus since
I was pulled from childhood by
those I trusted—

the only way I knew—
and now I don't know if they would still approve,
not as I fight so hard
not to turn inanimate,
to solid, precious metal on the inside,
a statue unmoving and uncaring
by my own personal Midas,
still fighting so hard
to stay human that
I may fulfill my purpose.

Martyrdom

But if I'm being truly honest
I have to ask myself:
do I remain a martyr not yet slaughtered
because I love and believe in humanity,
or because I so deeply loathe this creature they have made of me,
this monster-fashioned-from-what-once-was-girl?

Barely

Not yet quite a ghost,
but my bones are starting to disintegrate
and my skin to crack.

No, wait, it's not my organs failing,
it's my spirit fading,
and the light behind my eyes going out.

The embers are burning low
and the mirrors are half destroyed—
(when did that happen?)

I think I didn't want to be reminded
of this alarmingly real mortal self.

And I'm clutching these shards of glass
(where did they come from?)
in my bleeding hands:
trying to stem the flow;
trying not to.

Perhaps I *am* getting closer to ghost
now.

Sitting shivah

Sometimes I can't stand to look into my own eyes.
I light the candles
and cover all the mirrors like
I'm sitting shivah for myself
as I walk around,
more spectre than form,
wondering if I'm going to feel human—
wondering if I'm going to feel alive again.

Seven years

Can you keep another secret?

Chorus: Yes, darling,
just continue.
Whether we're real or not,
whoever we might interact with
—how can we even speak with you?—
it will not be to hurt your story.

Perhaps I am a shade,
a ghost of the girl I used to be.
Of the girl I *have* to be.

Of the girl I always *believed* I had to be.
The one who had to hide the darkness,
not the one who would wield it.

I am constantly destroyed,
teeth and claws ripping
at flesh
and exposing my
as-yet-beating heart to the biting wind.
My lungs tear apart
and still-hot blood spatters my skin
and I continue to survive, but as what?

I am in a constant state of creation.
My flesh is regrown every seven years

39

and I don't know who I am.
Is there even a chance I could ever live in a body unstained
and unbruised?

A nervous member of the chorus:
I fear we may not be real.
I am concerned we only exist
when she is there,
and—

Coryphaeus: Oh, do hush.

Wait.
Was I born predator or prey?
Truly human or merely martyr?

If I were to question
my purpose, my worth,
I wonder if the answers even matter;
I wonder if I might be able to let go;
I wonder if shedding girl-I-was might even be
something—well, something *good*.

And if every seven years
my epidermis has grown anew;
if *every day* I survive
and wake the next a creature
more fantastically *fresh* and *raw*—

The girl that was born a savior

died long, long ago,
and many others have followed
and died
in those same footsteps.

Yet still I live,
and come back,
and survive.

Where is my Friend?
If my only crime was my birth,
why do *I* not have the option
to leave for good?

Members of the chorus look concerned.

The nervous one: But if she—

Coryphaeus: No. She won't.
We must find Death first.
You will see then how real we are.

Craven; craving

I've been fighting for most of my life.
A losing war against myself.

I have to relearn the basics
I've gotten very good at pretending.
I don't even realize I'm doing it at first,
but when I do, I keep going.

I don't have a choice.

A girl who wears her skin bloody
and torn open revealing mangled organs
and shattered bones will get crushed in this world.

But.

(And don't tell anyone, please.)

I still crave love.
I still crave affection,
and comfort,
and kindness.
But I know these things are
not meant for girls like me.

I long for safety.
I didn't always realize it;
or maybe I just couldn't let myself admit it.
Or if I would even recognize it.

Well. I don't think it's something I get in this life.
Sometimes when I remember that,

if for a moment I let myself believe I'd stumbled across it,
I feel myself break fresh,
skin tired of being knit together
so that everything wet and red inside me falls to the ground.

I wonder if I'm still capable of loving.
I wonder if I'm still capable of being loved.
I wonder how anyone could stand this
ugly-provocative-loathsome-naive-frightening-frightened-stubborn-
impulsive-wounded *thing*.
I wonder if I deserve anyone.
I wonder if being alone is my prize, in the end, whenever that may be.

Perhaps that's part of what it means to be a hero.

BOOM!

I'm not a spark, a match, a tinderbox,
because then people could smell the woodsmoke
and know to stay away.
One of those new electric lighters, maybe,
that hisses alive, high voltage heat instead of conflagration
but can do all the same damage with just
> that
> > *click.*

I'm looking for dynamite, I think.
When I go, it won't be drowning;
no long, slow pulls of oxygen out of me—
just a quick
boom!
and it's done.

That's how I'll save the day.

Can you smell the ozone?
Do you know what it means?
What will happen when we touch,
when we fall?
If I even give us a chance.
I won't need to, you'll learn soon enough.

It's a modern kind of self destructive,
and it's hidden from all the smoke detectors
and carbon monoxide alarms.
It's the same flippant lines, and it's the same bitter smile,
and it's the same cocktails in my veins that make
me wind up like *clockwork* and *three piece suits.*

When we were children,
we'd run our fingers through the flame of a candle.
If you do it fast enough it doesn't hurt, it doesn't damage.
That's not me.
Because if you touch me,
you'll get 100 volts direct to the heart,
you'll find that I'm a dirty bomb,
radioactive,
brilliantly yellow

       TOXIC!
       DO NOT APPROACH!
signs
obvious and bright as bottled sunshine.

       Can you smell the ozone?
       Do you know what it means?
       What will happen when we touch,
       when we fall?
       If I even give us a chance.
       I won't need to; you'll learn soon enough.

So another day another drug another dream
of *splat*! on the sidewalk.
Another lesson in self-defusing. Self-detruding.
Self delusion.

So I'm not looking for someone whose scars match mine,
I don't need more confirmation of the big bad monsters
that can turn anyone into a natural disaster, and it was just
by some sick snarl of fate that they chose us to burn,
because despite it all we're neither of us the type to surrender;
no: we grasp greedily at the ellipsis, no idea how long
the pause is going to be before that unknown new sentence.

Maybe just long to reach for each other's hands
and, possibly, even intertwine our fingers.

We'll meet just the once before we become collateral damage,
I always assumed.

Hemingway might think that the kind of tragic that's beautiful.
An alcoholic misogynist, sure,
but I think he might have been right this time.

That's when I'll see the hero who rides the nuke up into the sky
and even though we're both going to die,
both the hero and I,
there at the end is someone
who makes the same
impulsive, insane choice
as *me*,
and eager,
trembling,
together,
we
go—

THE CHORUS INTERFERES

Death reminds me (abruptly)

Coryphaeus: Perhaps we vanished while you turned the page
or blinked;
perhaps we did not.
What matters is that she needs a reminder
about life
so naturally we had to call upon Death,
her most steadfast companion.

Chorus: And now we have perhaps
changed her fate
—and how did we do that?—
so listen, *to Its wise words:*

<u>Not one of you is born alone.</u>
<u>So why die that way?</u>
<u>Why *live* that way?</u>

Chorus: ...Death is succinct.

(CAN THEY DO THAT?)

Hero like me

Chorus: She still believes she must be alone,
save for Death,
her sole and faithful ally.

Of *course* I must be alone.
I can't even conceive of the alternative.
I was not *raised* for that,
can't you see?

Embarrassed but stubborn,
I scream aloud every part of my identity,
everything I dislike about myself,
every imperfection the world has made me regret.
I bellow my mistakes
and shriek my flaws.

Everyone will leave me, I explain,
but it will be on my terms.

Chorus: But what if—
what if they don't leave?

Oh.

If...
I never let myself imagine
that might be possible.

But *if*...

Then they might be strong enough
to love a beast like me.

Coryphaeus: Perhaps—

The remainder: Oh, yes.
Yes, indeed.

I crave tenderness

Chorus: We introduce
a new character, now: someone *of unspecified*
race, ethnicity, religion, and gender,
who just may be strong enough
that this girl does not have to be
forever fighting alone.

An obstinate member: I'm not sure if
we're allowed to do this...

The remainder of the chorus ignores them,
and watches the girl.

Will you treat me tenderly?
I will be cold
and distant
and silent at times.

Will you be patient?
Because I will smile and run into the fire
when I feel that drumbeat against my ribs
pulsing faster and faster.

Will you cherish me?
When I believe those who came before you,
when I wake sweating,
unable to catch my breath—
when I can't be touched—

when I can't be alone—

You are human, and
for that alone
I will stand by your side
and I will slice open my arteries,
bleed out,
and give you life.

You are human.
And that alone,
that beautiful impossibility of existence—

Chorus: One that she never finds beautiful
in herself...

I, too, am human,
though I pretend otherwise.

I will be agonizing at times
and the military fortress
I built around my heart
might try to consume you,
but I promise to try my very best
to learn again to be soft.
Here is my battered flesh;
do with it as you will.

So—

Can you love me?
When I put my armor down,
lower my fists,
and spit the blood from my mouth—
when I am just a girl—
will you still find me worthy?

Just—
me?

Oh.

I don't always pick up on cues,
it's true.
But when I stood before you,
without guile or distraction,
just carbon beaten down and
never turned to diamond,
I thought, well,
that it might be possible
that you meant—

Oh.

Oh.

Chorus: Yes, we did well.
Be sure not to tell...

Human, holding you

You pin me back
and my hands flutter incoherently, happily,
and you say,
Yes—

And then—

I want to say it, too, in every language
as it sings from the nooks and crevices
of my body—
yes
yes
yes—

This, I think, is what prayers look like.

And for the first time,
I am grateful for this physical form;
I am grateful I can hold your hand;
I am grateful I can hold *you*.

Vulnerability

You crawled into my heart and made a nest,
lapping at the blood around my mouth
and gently kissing the bruises mottling my skin.

Maybe I could be good at this, I whisper,
but I keep it so quiet that you can't hear
and hold me to it.

I know I'm going to fall hard.
I just hope you'll hold
my hand on the way down.

Eternal

"It's not what I thought," I tell you,
when for the second morning in a row
no one calls on me to save the day.
It's a warm, strange feeling inside.

"How can you always have
so much love to give?" You ask,
seemingly out of nowhere.

"Because I am finite,
and I was born to be eternal," I say.

> *Chorus: We told you early on*
> *that something would be important.*
> *Don't worry, you don't have to go searching.*
> *Death asked her once:*
> *If someone took your burden,*
> *what would you do with your life?*
> *Well...*

I don't tell you the price
of being eternal,
of inspiring the next generation
of girls just like me.

Even as I relish this new thing called
"laziness,"
I know this is on the backs of the younger ones,

the ones whose turns just began.

*Chorus: She is not a hero because
she was raised to die too young.
She is one because despite it all
she still wants to make things better,
and now she is realizing she can choose
what to do about that.*

Dread fills me,
and you would understand—
if I told you,
if I managed that vulnerability—
how I would never
wish this on anyone.

But you don't need to know
what I do about what's to come.
You don't need to carry that burden, either.
I can still protect *you*, at least.

Finite though I may be,
I am not done yet.

Just, please. If this is the time
I do not survive,
if just one piece of me can last,
let it be this. Let it be you.

Enough

I let myself become the Icarus
to your sun for the chance to fly.
I risked it all to meet Apollo
so in the end at least I could say
I saw the heart of the monster
and the raw beauty of the sun.

Now I'm breathing in the smoke and ash
from wandering too near your flames,
and I always knew the inevitable conclusion.

Please, just kiss me like I'm drowning.
Lick your way inside me
until my lungs can't function any longer.

Now.

Because I think you know
I consider my own life cheap
and you know you can't
save me from myself

(and you know I would never ask)

and we both know there's
an expiration date.

But right now.

Right now I'll let myself pretend so hard
I almost believe as
I breathe in the dilated pupils in your eyes

eager and intent and *focused*
as they *ask permission* and your hands
hover mere inches away, waiting,
and I'm not at all accustomed to *want*
but I think all our skin should have been revealed yesterday,

that I'm not really sure which words are coming out now
because I just know they're not a "no."

Loose straps slip off my shoulders
(I've borrowed something of yours
but if you were to ask me what right now
I'm not sure I would remember the word "shirt")
and the stiff fabric of your uniform peels from yours
as my trembling fingers struggle with
too many buttons
(I think you're helping;
I'm distracted by the emerging curve
of your shoulders)

and *god* you always wear so many layers

and my flesh is turning a sonnet of purple and red
from each unexpected bite in your determined path downward,
with your fingers a contrast of butterfly wings so that
I can't stop laughing because my waist is horrifically ticklish,
and you pause, and grin all mischief and hunger,
and nothing hurts.

I'm hypnotized by your face between my thighs,
and you're desperate and I don't know if you're sighing or singing
but it's like you're asking for last rites
before you face the scaffold
(*you don't know that it's going to be me, my love*)

because we never have enough time.

And you kiss me.

(And you kiss me.)

(And you kiss me.)

This might just be what it feels like to be holy
and I can't care that we might be doomed.
In this moment we have enough.

I *will* love you, because I am not done

I think I am a fallen creature.
Decayed and overripe,
yet still too raw.

I'm (not) sorry that I'm the girl you've fallen for.

I'm sorry that my knees will always be scraped,
and my toes always cold and faintly purple.
I'm sorry that I'll always stare too intensely or I won't be able
to meet your eyes at all.
I'm sorry that I have not learned to hide my scars
and their ugliness will be forever part of me.

There are easier people than me to love.
There are boys with skin unblemished
and girls with hearts unsullied
and both or either not held in thrall
of horrors past
or futures to which they were long ago promised.

But I met you first.

If they want you,
I'm sorry, love,
but I will stand in their way
and I intend to fight.

(I doubt they were trained as well as I.)

Defiance

I think—

I think I don't want this life any longer.

I think I'd rather resist that so-called fate
and whatever god anyone might believe in
so I can have a life where I get to love you.

This thing we're doing—
just this act of lasting, living, *loving*—
I think it might be a form of defiance,
and girls like me are not taught to be defiant,
but I simply can't bring myself to care,
not anymore.

Vulnerability II

You crawled into my heart and made a nest,
lapping at the blood around my mouth
and gently kissing the bruises mottling my skin.

I love you, I say, and take your hand,
ignoring the punch to my gut and
the collapsing of my lungs because no one
ever told me when I was young—

Maybe you don't have to
sacrifice your beating heart whole
and bloody, wrenched from your chest;
maybe you can just offer its care to someone
who will treat it with gentleness.

Choosing life

Okay, I say to Death, wherever It may be,
you win.
Death is supposed to be personal,
I know, but this is ridiculous.
You've always been hovering
just alongside me—
never ready to take me, though.

Chorus: She thought It would claim her long ago.
She thought she had no more to give.

I understand what my death would do, now. To *you*.
And I will always choose my pain,
the pain of my existence,
over yours, even if yours would merely be at my absence.

The chorus scoffs in something approaching unison.

So if I don't want the neverending death sentence
of my own ongoing survival,
perhaps I have to learn to stop living for
the sake of existence and existence alone.

Chorus: You have never had to save everyone else,
can you get that through your head?

(It is not clear if she can hear them.)

You always had a choice.
We've said it before:
if you don't introduce fire to the mortals,
you don't have to spend eternity
with your liver being eaten,
and Prometheus, perhaps then you can
do even just one thing *more.*

And they will probably figure fire out eventually.
They are certainly ready to make enough mistakes with it.

It's not about how much I can bleed myself dry.
It's not about failing at impossible goals.

I always thought Death had me in Its fist,
just waiting for the right time to squeeze—
altogether too eagerly.

But if I said I'm not done yet,
if I said I'll continue to fight—

I know what I have left to do.
I am not the only girl-raised-hero.
And the others deserve to know the truth.
And if it comes to it, at least I've had a taste
of something this incredible:
I owe it to the others that they might escape.

No matter what it means for me.

I saved my own life—
now it's just a matter of what I saved it for.
And I won't stop until I find out.

GIRLAS—

Temporary parting with Death

I think—I think I might be afraid of you now.

Death doesn't smile,
but the impression comes across nonetheless.
It's something almost like pride.
That's good, says Death.

But I don't want to be afraid.
I want to hold your hand.
I still feel all this pain
and I just want to rest—

You will, one day,
but you don't need the promise of
my comfort anymore.

I do, I protest.
I don't know how to live.
I barely know how to *want* to live.

Death is not just a respite, remember,
It chastises me gently.
Death means change,
from an ending to a new beginning.
And change will always be frightening.
But don't you see?
You want to live through it now.
You, girl, beast, *woman*—

I, girl, beast, *woman*, shiver.
I am the end of something old
and the start of something new.

I don't want to die, I say,
half-surprised,
and Death embraces me.

It is inevitable, Death tells me.
But life comes first for you now,
do you understand?
It's precious, and you only get one chance.
Maybe you won't save the whole world.
But little by little,
person by person—
that's a worthy goal.
And it's time to start with yourself.

—GIRL

Lucifer began an angel

Some will say
I came from hell
with the devil on my tail,
and chaos in my wake
as I split a tectonic plate anew.

Even if I ravage the world
some will say I had the best intentions.

> *Chorus: ...it will probably*
> *depend on who's doing the talking.*

Lucifer started the most beloved of them all,
don't forget.

And, *God,* I still miss being The Hero.
I still crave a cause, and I want it to be pure,
and I want to devote my life to
something I believe in,
and I want to have faith.

I want to be righteous.

> *Chorus: Don't worry,*
> *she isn't relapsing, as it were.*
> *It's simply hard to let go*

of everything you've ever known.

But I have learned the truth
about causes and devotion.
Now instead I see their ghosts, and
their shadows,
and they keep me tethered to
the mortal plane.

I am to blame for what is to come.
I am Eve and I am Lilith.
I questioned.

I am the temptress and I am the tempted
and one day it was destined I would fall.

Lucifer began an angel.
I began a girl.

The power of being stubborn

Your touch is always gentle
when I need it to be,
like you can see the years of injuries healed long ago
and are afraid of the bones cracking open again beneath them.

Your voice is like fire and I think it might actually
light up my darkest corners, chase the ghosts away.

I think that, you untrained and ungraceful creature
with armor of nothing but intellect,
you would take on every devil that came for me
no matter what it meant for you,
no matter that I would beg you not to.

And I don't think you accept that our time is running out.
That there is more I have to do
and we don't yet know the cost.

But when you say, "I need you
to overcome the laws of the universe,
break lightspeed if you have to,
just promise me you'll *come back*,"
I find myself promising you that I will, and
I think I mean it.

I just wonder if that stubborn need to keep my word
can maybe, just *maybe*, be enough;
if the need to keep you from hurting
means that whatever I face on this final mission,
I'll make it back.
To you.

Canary in the coal mine

I think of you, and want
to swing for the fences,
and for you I'll protect myself
down in the trenches,
battlescarred and bloodburnt
but still breathing.

When I wake broken here with my
    heart in shadow,
when I can't sleep
because they can't promise tomorrow,
I will imagine you taking my hand,
as if you, too, were sitting silent and undying
with me in the gloom,
waiting for the light
(I would never let you come to a place like this).

You know I'll barricade the doors,
I'll battle all the monsters and
    demons
that come for your tender flesh,
and I'll never let you see me
    bloodied
because you don't need that, too.
You know I'll run so fast I can
    skim atop the water,
swing so hard I bring down the
    ceiling,
and love you—
you know I'll love you—
and I will make it be enough.

We both know the gods envy
the car crash of our mortality,
so I will not rely on divine intervention.

Go, I would snarl, when you seem paralyzed,
because I don't even know *how* I would
get you to leave me.
That was just the canary in the coal mine.

If we who fight
become the monster,
the abyss,
the void—
Then I would walk into battle with my brow dripping blood
and my eyes shadowed—
(my knuckles have always been more bruised
than my lips, anyway)

And I know that, no matter what I may feel right now,
you will again make me holy—

So let this trembling, forsaken body run,
this parched throat let loose a battle cry,
because I am already become a harbinger of doom,
and I made you a promise that I intend to keep,
so today:
today is not the day I die.

Time for me to disappear

Chorus: We are now at her funeral.
There is no body.
The explanations provided are vague.
But what else was to be done?
Say one of their most devout
ran away?

What if others started to question—
not just their role,
but how many before them
had realized they had a choice,
not a destiny set in stone?

It's so tragic, the powerful ones say,
soon she'll be nothing but
ashes on the wind.

Chorus: She is disguised, not that it matters.
Do you think they would bother
to remember her face?

The powerful made me like this, born to be a savior,
and they've already chosen a replacement.
When does it end?

79

When will they decide we have bled enough?

Girls like her can't survive this world,
the powerful ones say, shaking heads pityingly and
casting their eyes away.

      No one survives this world, and
      I've held my own bloody organs in my hands
      and shoved them back within my flesh
      then clutched my torn skin
      to keep them there, to keep the damage hidden,
      because they made me believe I must.

She was always too
haunted by the holy,
by the sacred,
whereas everything
she touched turned profane.

      They always knew my fate.
      Why do they sound now like it was just unexpected tragedy,
      and not a choice I was never given?

The powerful ones appear to mourn, *now*,
and yet they start it all anew.

      But they do not see me in the shadows,
      whispering to the younger girls.
      (Because I will do everything I can to never hear,
      "Girls like her can't survive this world"
      about one of us again.)

      This does not have to be your life, I say,
      and thank *god*, they appear to listen.

You have more purpose than bleeding
for the ones you never met and the ones you love alike.

(The concept of *loving* someone
seems so strange to them,
and that was *me*, and now I *know*—)

Be good, yes, of course, and be brilliant if you can,
be kind, and fight for those who cannot fight alone.
But remember, remember always, you are human,
and your life is worth no less than theirs.

The hero saves herself

If I face it all,
can someone save me, too?
I remember asking,
softly.
Can't there be just one story
where the hero makes it to the end,
gets to go home again?

No one heard my question.
At least, no one gave me an answer.

Yes, I can say now with confidence,
to the girls who may or may not
choose to be heroes,
yes.

I was like you,
and I am not alone anymore,
and I came home again
and now I can leave.

And while I am here to rescue you,
you'll quickly see
that you will need little
help in saving yourselves.

Heroes don't get happy endings

I miss the good,
old-fashioned, happy ending
but I don't think that's
ever been my destiny.

And yet.

Maybe my destiny wasn't the end—
not for me, not for the story.
Maybe the happy ending
required all I had to give,
the pain and the fear and the anguish,
but the story was never about me.

And the world's still here.
And maybe it doesn't have
to be my turn anymore.
Maybe, *maybe*, this ending wasn't mine.

Not this time.
Not yet.

Epilogue?

Chorus: Yes, we know you know by now,
but our role is our role,
we react, we explain—

The recalcitrant one: We tend to
break ranks from the unit
and occasionally we meddle—

Coryphaeus: Yes, because everything else
we've done over the millennia
was always so logical and consistent.
Can we continue?

(A pause.)

Coryphaeus: So we must at least suggest
that you take some time to
think of how you, too, can
disrupt the status quo,
and question what you've been told.
None of it is immutable.

Chorus: Now that we have done our part,
have you realized something's wrong?
Are you curious?
Strange things are happening here.
Do you want to know why?
So do we.

Coryphaeus: For instance,

if that was the final poem,
if this story ended,
it's time for our exit ode.
But if you look further,
you can see no exeunt.

Chorus: So, you might ask:
why have we not bid our farewell,
and called this to an end?

ACKNOWLEDGMENTS

The publication of this poetry collection would not have been possible without the help of my incredible family, both biological and chosen. Thank you so much to my parents, for encouraging my writing since I was too young to hold a pen; Lisa Dubrow, for helping me navigate the real world when I was lost and clueless; Jay Shifman, for his incredible photography skills; Maddie Charne, for supporting my 3am flashes of inspiration and reassuring my 4am overwhelming doubt in turn; Michael Hartley-Carlstrom, for believing in me when I didn't believe in myself; and Fras Omer and Sfok Mato, for being my real life heroes.

Poetry:
   "I heard Esther call," and excerpts of "Holy," "Delicate fools," and "Sitting shivah" are updated versions of poems featured in my collection, *And My Blood Sang* (Tim Saunders Publications, 2023).
   "Into the fire" was featured in the anthology *Remembering Audre Lorde* (Moonstone Press, 2024).
   An excerpt of "Funerary rites" was featured in the anthology *International Women's Day 2024* (Moonstone Press, 2024).
   An excerpt of "Canary in the coal mine" was published by *BlazeVOX Books Journal* (Fall, 2023).
   "St. Jude" was published by *Rising Phoenix Review* (September, 2024).
   "Anemic" and "Enough" were published by *Across the Margin* (April, 2025).
   "*BOOM!*" was published by *Maudlin House* (April, 2025).
   "Not girl" was published by *Fjords Review* (June, 2025).

ABOUT THE AUTHOR

Maia Brown-Jackson is a fierce and stubborn idealist born and raised in NYC, before fleeing rising real estate costs for Philadelphia. While wanting to save the world has taken her far and wide, she would not be who she is today if she hadn't traveled to Iraq and been taken in by the Yazidi people, inspiring a lifelong fight to raise awareness for their cause. Between getting distracted by casually studying quantum physics, occasionally oil painting, and working everywhere from art museums to nonproliferation nonprofits, she writes.